Tell Me About
Love

Published in Nashville, Tennessee, by Tommy Nelson®, a Division of Thomas Nelson, Inc.

Tommy Nelson® books may be purchased in bulk for educational, business, fund-raising, or sales promotional use. For information, please email SpecialMarkets@ThomasNelson.com.

Scripture quotations in this book are from the *International Children's Bible*®, *New Century Version*®, © 1986, 1988, 1999 by Tommy Nelson®, a Division of Thomas Nelson, Inc. All rights reserved.

Library of Congress Cataloging-in-Publication Data

Anderson, Joel.
  Tell me about love / by Joel Anderson ; illustrated by Joel Anderson
and Kristi Carter Smith.
      p. cm. — (Big topics for little kids)
  ISBN 1-4003-0616-7 (hardcover)
  1. Love—Religious aspects — Christianity — Juvenile literature. I. Smith, Kristi Carter.
II. Title.
  BV4639.A535 2005
  241'4—dc22

                                    2005000012

Printed in China

05 06 07 08 09 RRD 5 4 3 2 1

big topics for little kids™

Tell Me About Love

by Joel Anderson

Illustrated by Joel Anderson
and Kristi Carter Smith

Tommy
NELSON®

www.tommynelson.com

A Division of Thomas Nelson, Inc.
www.ThomasNelson.com

Love is patient and kind.
Love is not jealous, it does not brag,
and it is not proud. Love is not rude,
is not selfish, and does not become angry
easily. Love does not remember wrongs
done against it. Love is not happy with
evil, but is happy with the truth. . . .
Love never ends.

1 CORINTHIANS 13:4–8

It was a sad day for some
thankful people.

Their home was gone.

But they were glad to have one another.

They were still alive,
thanks to one member of the family.

This family member
had been given a great gift—
a home and the love of a family.

And she had given her family an even greater gift in return.

The family thought about
the first time they met her.

She was lost and scared.
She was dirty and hungry.

Her new family
gave her a bath,
a bed, and
plenty of food.

And she grew to love them all.

Every day she would
greet them.

Every night she would
stay close to protect them.

She was happy to belong to them.
They were glad to be her family.

Then came the night that changed their lives forever.

It was dark and quiet. Something didn't smell right.
She knew she had to wake the family.

She did not stop barking
until everyone was out of the burning house.

They stood safely outside and waited for her.
But she never came out.

They had given her a family.
She had given them her life.

As they said good-bye, they were very thankful
for the one thing that would always remain,
even after it had been given away. . . .

. . . the gift of love.

*This is how we know
what real love is:
Jesus gave his life for us.*

1 JOHN 3:16

Parent / Teacher Discussion Aid

Q. Does someone have to die to show love?

A. No. There are many ways to show love by helping, sharing, and caring for others. Love is more than just a feeling. Love is a choice. When you love someone, you choose to do what's best for them. The dog in the story loved her family so much that she lost her life while trying to save them. But that's just one way she loved her family. Any time you put someone's needs in front of your own, you are showing love. Especially if you do not want to get something back from them. To show love to others, you might let someone get in front of you in line, or you might make a card or do something helpful to show another person that you care. Love is shown by your actions and words.

Q. Are there different kinds of love?

A. Yes, there are several different kinds of love. The love of best friends is different from the love of parents and children. The love of mommies and daddies is different from the love you might have for your country. God's love is the most perfect love there is. In fact, the Bible says that God is Love.

Q. How do you know if someone loves you?

A. When someone loves you, they like to be with you. And they do things that are good for you. Your parents show their love when they feed you, give you a safe place to live, think about you often, take care of you when you are sick, and give you gifts on special days. A teacher may show love for you by making sure you are learning and growing. A friend may show love for you by helping you, playing with you, listening to you, and forgiving you.

Q. How does God show His love for us?

A. Even before we could love God, He loved us first. He sent Jesus, His one and only Son, to die for our sins, so that if we believe in Him, our sins are forgiven and we can live forever with God in heaven. God shows us His love by sending rain and sunshine to care for His creation. He paints the skies in beautiful colors with sunsets and rainbows to show us His love. God also gave us His Word, the Bible, to tell us all about His love.

Q. How should we treat people who do not love us?

A. Jesus said we should love those who do not love us back. When we are kind only to nice people, we are not showing a lot of love. But when someone has been selfish or mean to us, we have a chance to show God's kind of love by forgiving them and being kind in return. This kind of love is hard. We have to ask God to fill our heart with special love—the kind only He can give. When we love other people with the love God gives us, we are like a light, shining to the world. And when people see our good deeds, they will praise our Father in heaven.

Experiment for Little People

Name three people who love you.
Tell how you know they love you.

Name three people you love.
How do you show your love to them?

Try to show love to the people you named in each of these four ways:
1. with a hug
2. with kind words
3. with a good deed
4. with a small gift

Try to do this every day! Practice loving someone by treating them even better than you would want to be treated. Be generous. You will find that loving others brings joy. Love changes them and you. Love will fill both of you with joy and make life beautiful.